HOW YOU SEE IT

The Power of Perspective

B.Lin

Cover designed by Justin M. Carey Designs

Printed in the United States of America

First Printing: August 2020
The Scribe Tribe Publishing Group
P.O. Box 1264 Homewood, IL 60430

THE SCRIBE TRIBE
PUBLISHING GROUP

ISBN-978-1-7352568-0-1

This book is dedicated to anyone determined to find the bright side.

CONTENTS

INTRODUCTION

As I watch the world go into versions of quarantine over COVID-19, we have one or two options. We can either panic or reset. Doesn't life offer these options more often than not? What's funny is that this is the third introduction I've written, but the one that feels most necessary.

I've been looking for a way to get my point across. Whether I'm writing and erasing or typing and deleting, I know what I'm TRYING to say. It is my hope that the thoughts expressed will positively influence the way you see things. With that being said, I believe that the best way to connect is through relatability.

It turns out that the Coronavirus pandemic is something everyone has in common. If you're anything like me, I'd rather us just have the same favorite show, but that's not how the world works. Unfortunately, we are both a part of a scary moment in history. I've watched multiple sides be taken because of this virus. Regardless of who's behind it, we can all agree that it is a wakeup call.

Consider the way we've bombarded the grocery stores. I've never seen the cleaning aisle so clear or options so scarce in the food department. Most people are viewing this as the end of the world. However, it seems to me that this virus has reinforced cleanliness, home-cooked meals, and even prayer. One could argue this being the beginning of a better world.

While we don't know how long this will last, watching the world pause has been eye-opening. Have we been in such a rush that we've lost sight of a few values? If the world ended, are we happy with what we've accomplished thus far? Will we sleep the days away or dive into new discoveries? Your life is a result of what you do with your time.

Whether it's a virus or a car accident, life has a way of getting our attention. By the time you read this, I hope the spread of COVID-19 will be over and that the world will have a new and improved normal. I had a choice between watching a movie and putting some order to my book. I hope it's obvious which option I chose.

THE GLASS

Is the glass half empty or is it half full?

Do you care about the water or does the glass rule?

Can it even fill you up?

Is the water even cool?

Is the glass too heavy?

Can the water not improve?

At least you got a glass though,

Some use hands.

Some make the music and some just dance.

Some think big and some think small.

Some just text, but some still call.

You ever take a sip and just think for a second?

Pour a glass of water, it'll teach you a lesson.

-B.Lin

PERSPECTIVE

I magine pouring the same amount of water into two different glasses. One is short and round while the other is tall and thin. Most people would gravitate toward the taller glass because they would assume it had more in it. I'm sure you've heard of the classic glass analogy where the amount in the glass is based on perspective. If you see the glass as half empty, you'll always want more. If you see the glass as half full, you'll always have **enough.**

Let's look at the word "enough." This word is often used in two extremely popular ways: good enough or more than enough. When viewing something as good enough, it almost sounds like settling.

When viewing something as more than enough, it sounds like extreme fulfillment. The average dictionary might suggest that for something to be enough means that it is a sufficient amount. It is interesting how the intent for something could be positive yet received negatively.

Did you know that one negative thought could turn into ten negative thoughts? Have you ever realized that a positive mindset creates a better reality? It is no secret that everything we are and have is the sum of our thought process. You **deserve** the mindset you've always wanted. I can't wait until you realize the power of perspective.

LIFE vs. DEATH

Tomorrow is a luxury, and your destiny is **fragile**. Each day we wake up is a new opportunity to show our appreciation for life. The best way to do this is to give 100% effort in all you do. Whether it is work or a day off, strive to display high performance as a person.

Let each conversation you have end positively. Find reasons to smile and be sure to have a day that you enjoyed.

Death and decisions are two things we can't escape. Never assume that you'll have another chance. Decisions determine destiny. Your destiny gets altered when you avoid evolving. We must be careful with the way we respond to life.

We exist because we have been perfectly designed by God to fulfill purpose on earth. When you understand life, then you'll understand death. Live a life you'd be at peace with if it ended suddenly. Whether it be character or accomplishments, be proud of who you are and what you do while you're here. Your **legacy** will be a result of these two factors.

~R.I.P. Kobe & GiGi~

CHOICES

Some time ago, I was trying to make an important decision. The result was going to determine the next season of my life. I asked a friend for advice, and she lovingly told me that I had a **choice** between two paths. Simply put, she said that one path would be that of comfort, and the other would be that of discomfort. This scenario applies to you as much as me.

When considering the path of comfort, know that it usually consists of what you're used to or what would be easy. When considering the path of discomfort, know that it will consist of risks and unfamiliarity. If you do what you've always done, the results will be what they've always been. Doing something new is the only way to guarantee different results.

At the end of the day, our fate is influenced by the choices we make. The deciding factor is based upon the pick of the path. You can do what you've always done, but wouldn't that be boring? After all, you wouldn't be reading this if something inside of you didn't long for more.

ROCK BOTTOM

Sometimes all you have left is what God puts **inside** of you, not what's in front of you. You begin to question why you're even here when you're looking at fear, disappointment, or regret. This kind of circumstance can make or break your destiny. In fact, when you've hit rock bottom, you can only either stay down or get up.

Keep in mind the things that make you happy. Not people, but things. The hidden talents that help you escape don't have to stay hidden. What have you always wanted to do? The dreams that are inside of you are glimpses of your potential reality.

Don't let a rough day turn into a rough season or a rough season turn into a rough life. Get in tune with your happy place and stay there. Develop what you're good at, even if you're nervous. Rock bottom was only ever meant to **reroute** you to the top.

WORK ETHIC

When they say, "keep your eye on the prize," they really mean keep your **mind** on the prize. You have to see it before you see it. The only thing that can bring vision to life is focus. The only thing that can shape your focus is mentality. The difference between possible and impossible is your **work ethic**.

You must know what you want to go about achieving it. The end goal is most achievable when the vision is clear. Once the vision is clear, there should be a shift in mindset. Some people work harder in their dreams than they do in real life. I was one of those people until I realized I was more successful when I was awake than when I was asleep.

Dreaming is cool but doing is much better. This is why Nike, one of the world's largest brands, encourages us to "Just Do It." This usually works for those who are brave enough to focus. When your mentality is to succeed, that's exactly what you'll do. Stop at nothing to adopt the mindset of a winner.

DOUBT

Often, we doubt our own greatness. Successful people have mentioned that there is only 1 percent of those who will live up to their fullest potential. For some reason, the average person prefers to settle for safe. This is the only way they can control their narrative, though the outcome may be **mediocre**.

Why do we do this? When you imagine the unimaginable and think the unthinkable, it can feel both terrifying and exciting. Those that are terrified either fear the process, people's opinions, or their qualifications for what they see in their minds. Those that feel excited have enough **faith** to take the steps necessary to see their dream come true. Which one are you?

Go for your dream, even if nobody sees what you see. Playing it safe will only produce **regret**. You don't deserve to be familiar with that emotion. If you have to ask yourself, "what if it doesn't work out?" Make sure the answer is, "what if it does?"

EXPOSURE

Hear me when I say this. You met them for a reason, you saw that for a reason, and you know it for a reason. **Nothing** we experience is by accident. Albert Einstein once said that imagination is the preview of life's coming attractions. I'd like to follow up with saying that exposure is proof of life's **possibilities**.

Have you ever met someone that became something extraordinary? Perhaps when you met them, their dream seemed difficult, but as time went on, it became their reality. Consider your favorite teacher, friend, or even stranger that changed your perspective on dreams.

What once seemed scary suddenly became exciting. Exposure is not a coincidence.

Had you not encountered those people, you may not have seen what it takes for you to know what you could become. If you didn't attend that school, join that program, or walk in that building, that experience wouldn't exist in your life. Without exposure, there'd be no experience. Allow exposure to **enhance** your drive and watch what happens.

EVENTUALLY

Do you ever find yourself waiting for something that seems far away? This usually happens when you feel like you've been waiting for a long time. We only look forward to what we believe we deserve. Waiting **seems** absurd when you've come up with reasons for why you should have something already.

Two things undoubtedly make dreams come true: your work ethic and God's timing. If your desires are based on skillset and natural abilities, all you need is a **plan** and consistency. Nothing is impossible when talent and ambition join forces. Think about the last time something happened later than anticipated, but exactly when it should have.

When it comes to God's timing, know that he has everything under control. Sometimes we need lessons to appreciate blessings. The most successful people are familiar with failure. As long as you're doing your best, simply be ready. Your moment is closer than you realize. It may not have happened yet, but **eventually,** it will.

SUCCESS

TALENTS vs. GIFTS

I f you're good at something, you should be found doing it. Our purpose is the sum total of our gifts. Many people spend their entire lives **looking** for purpose when it is actually hiding in **plain sight.** Where talents need training, gifts flow naturally. We tend to gravitate more toward skill sets rather than natural ability. However, using your gifts could open doors for more purpose than you imagined.

Make sure you understand the difference between talents and gifts. Michael Jordan was an extremely talented basketball player, but his gift was in the **creativity** of his skill. This same creative mind allowed him to merge athletics and fashion into what is one of the largest brands to this day. Ultimately, it is his creativity that makes him one of the greatest successes on and off the court.

We must give our gifts the attention they deserve so that we can experience the life that was written for us. Know that anything that comes naturally is a field you should explore. Talents come in seasons, but gifts never leave. The best part about gifts is that we all have more than one. We must look beyond the surface to see them.

CONSISTENCY

Anything you aspire to develop takes **consistency**. Consider the life span of a flower. Once you plant the seed, it takes water for it to grow. If you water it once, it'll still be a seed, but if you water it daily, it will develop into a blooming flower.

I once received roses on a date. They were so beautiful that I immediately put them in water and set them on the table for everyone to see. While I initially marveled at their beauty, I failed to **nourish** them, and they died a few days later. Oftentimes, we let ideas slip away because we don't take the time to nourish them. Don't spend more time focusing on what you have than on the work it takes to keep it.

The worst thing you can do for something you love is nothing at all. Hard work truly **does** pay off. Only those that are successful will equate hard work to consistency. Anything promising deserves attention. The only way to get better is to do a little each day until it becomes second nature to grow.

OBSTACLES

What seems to be in the way is what helps **pave** the way. Obstacles are inevitable on the road of opportunity. You just have to decide which "O" you will focus on. To get to something, you must go through something. This is the only road that leads to success.

Imagine driving at your desired speed limit, only to be interrupted by a pothole. Not only is this interruption annoying, but it could also ruin your tires if you aren't careful. Often, we can't see what's in front of us because we aren't **pacing** ourselves. The only way you can adjust to the interruption is to avoid thinking that it doesn't exist.

Obstacles vs. Opportunity is a never-ending war. Opportunity wins the war when it uses **strategy** to defeat the obstacle in its way. Strategy can only be found through focus. As you navigate through life, know that true success always comes with a fight. When you accept this truth, only then will you overcome what you couldn't avoid.

VISION

Never lose sight of what you see in your mind. Vision is always attached to a **purpose**. There is no way God would allow your imagination to tease you if what you saw couldn't manifest. The only way we will get anywhere is by working toward our vision. The only way to work toward vision is to have a plan.

By setting a plan, you are proving to yourself that you're ready to act. By taking action, you are proving to God that you're ready for him to take **control**. If you spend your life only dreaming, then you've already died. You must invest just as much in your abilities as you do your imagination.

Take your vision seriously. Try to consider your dreams as you would a payment **loan**. Just as someone loans you money to achieve a goal, God loans you vision to achieve purpose. What you produce through your plan is the way you pay him back. Wouldn't you like to see what happens when you give it all you've got?

SUCCESS

When success is mentioned, most people equate it to having accomplished a career aspiration. Most times, we **assume** that to be successful, one must have multiple streams of income or a large salary. Obtaining a lot of money seems to be the end goal for many. What if success has nothing to do with the money?

To me, you're successful when you're giving life your best efforts. You're successful when you're **happy**. You're successful when you're good to people. You're successful when you treat your health with respect. You're successful when you lead with faith.

Reconsider the way you view success. It looks different to everyone. Decide what would make your life better and strive toward that. Let no one define it but you. Ignore society's attempts to pressure you into its idea of success. Perhaps it is more than what meets the eye and the wallet.

RELATIONSHIPS

ROMANTIC BREAKUP

You've just spent a chunk of time getting to know someone. You learned how to love them and **invested** energy into making the most of your relationship. For some reason, things just didn't seem to work out. If we're honest, you may have even seen this coming but didn't want to accept it.

What now? I'll tell you what... You've just had a **real** experience. Every time you get into a new relationship, you are taking a risk on a love that may or may not last. To have a real experience takes a real risk. Some people spend their entire lives being afraid of love. Be proud that your heart has the **capacity** to invest in another human being in such a vulnerable way.

Allow yourself permission to endure the emotions of breakups. There is a lesson behind everything that you feel. Don't let a breakup turn into a breakdown. You didn't lose anything that can't be replaced with something better. If it was over before it ended, no need to regret it. If it caught you off guard, may it bring you closer to yourself. A breakup with them can be a make-up with you.

FRIENDSHIP BREAKUP

Nothing hurts worse than friendship breakups. If you're really close, they may have even become family. Many times, friends feel like the soulmates we've always wanted. When a bond like this comes to an end, losing that friend can feel like losing yourself.

Be careful **not** to retaliate. The demise of friendship could bring about very upsetting emotions. While it's hard to accept a new fate, it's even harder to forget the one you had in mind. No longer being friends doesn't erase that they were once important to you. Accept your present and **respect** your past.

There is still beauty in loss. You gained great experience with someone who probably gave you some of your **best** memories. Remember the bond before you respond. You probably wouldn't be who you are without having loved this friend. Some last a lifetime and some are seasonal, but every season makes the lifetime **worthwhile**.

EXPECTATIONS

The only expectation you should set is for yourself. It is both unrealistic and **unfair** to assume that a person knows how to be a certain way. You are only responsible for your role in any relationship. Human beings will make a lot more sense when you accept this.

Have you ever been disappointed by someone you love? This disappointment stems from you not expecting people you're close with to hurt you. Sometimes we give a person **permission** to hurt us when we view them as superhuman. Just because someone loves you doesn't mean they'll present a perfect display of that love.

Every human being is flawed. At most, you can only hope that those you let into your life will have good intentions. Make sure you have them as well because you are also **capable** of disappointment. The reality is that the world is full of imperfect people who want to be accepted for who they are. Love will get a lot bigger when you get rid of your expectations.

EGO

"It's important that I'm always right."

"I love you, but I'm going to ignore you to prove a point."

"I'm the best you'll ever have."

Listed above are some of the ego's favorite thoughts. They are also some of the ego's most **toxic** thoughts. One of the worst things you can do is let self-importance ruin your opportunity to grow with someone. You must be uncomfortable to grow. This means that things cannot only go your way.

The ego is to blame for many open wounds. Rather it is an argument, a misinterpreted text, or insecurity posing as confidence;

these unresolved issues can stem from the nature of the ego. It loves to protect itself and doesn't like to lose. We all know what happens to open wounds. When a situation isn't treated properly, it can **infect** the relationship and affect the outcome.

Before leading with ego, consider how much someone or something means to you. Pride can ruin potential improvement. Try assessing a matter for what it is as opposed to how you want it to be. Silencing the ego is much better than controlling the narrative. You're sure to have positive results when you navigate **selflessly**.

BOUNDARIES

Too much of anything is just that...too much. It is particularly important to know the **difference** between healthy vs. excessive. A healthy amount of involvement will lead to success. An excessive amount could lead to disaster. Being obsessed with something can distract you from other areas that deserve your attention.

Boundaries represent the limits you set in place for successful results. If you are dating someone, it is quite easy to become addicted to this person. Setting limits to your involvement will stop you from losing yourself along the way. The same applies to friendships. If you are voluntarily consumed with another human being, you may develop certain habits that **harm** the relationship.

In a nutshell, boundaries prevent regret. This kind of self-control proves your commitment to a more positive outcome. There's a lot to be said about a person who understands how to **balance** their life. You can only experience the sanity that comes with balance when you grasp the concept of boundaries.

CHARACTER

INTENT

Intentions determine results. Your intent represents how you really feel regardless of your actions. Have you ever pursued an opportunity because it was good, but not because you really wanted it? Have you ever dated someone for what they could do instead of how they made you feel? Have you ever befriended someone for what they had as opposed to who they were?

We don't have to pretend like any of these had a happy ending. When your intentions aren't **genuine**, you will not have success.

Pursue what makes you happy, not what feeds your ego. You'll have to work twice as hard to fool others because fooling yourself will only eat you alive. I think our best bet is to just be real.

If you question your intent, ask yourself why you're doing something. Self-transparency is **essential** for honest reflection. How you manage your intentions is a direct reflection on your character.

GOSSIP

We have all been **guilty** of talking too much. Whether you've shared another's secret or made a verbal assumption about someone, it still qualifies as **gossip**. The thing about gossip is that it exposes a reality about your character. You either enjoy bringing people down, or you aren't brave enough to not participate when others do it. Here's a harsh truth: If you're listening, you're still participating.

The good thing about gossiping is that you know how to talk about more than just yourself. The bad thing about gossiping is that there really **isn't** a good thing. I just didn't want you to feel bad. People who have this immediate ability to discuss others negatively, subconsciously just want to know that they aren't the only ones with issues. Those who are focused on solving their own issues have little time to focus on everyone else's.

The next time you see an opportunity to gossip, view it as **compromising**. Instead of worrying about the bond you have with someone else, consider the bond you have with yourself. Stop at nothing to improve in character, even if it means sacrificing relationships.

HELP

People come into your life for one or two reasons: For you to get something from them or for them to get something from you. Each of us has something to **contribute** to the world. You can positively influence someone's weakness by using one of your strengths. When the word "help" is mentioned, most people automatically think of money. However, help can also consist of physical assistance, prayer, and so much more.

Consider a homeless person. I know it isn't always easy to tell if they are really in need. I imagine it is difficult and even embarrassing to even position yourself to beg. At the very least, they need kind words and empathy. The smallest **gesture** can make the biggest impact.

We have all been blessed with a **heart**. It is not recommended that you be selfish with yours. If you have the means to help, go ahead and help. You cannot predict how people will respond to your display of service. Let love lead you. Last time I checked, it's better to give than receive.

NEVER AGAIN

The only way to stop a bad habit is to just **stop**. How you learn something is exactly how you can unlearn it. Our behavior is a result of our habits. If you're tired of an outcome that you can control, change your role in the narrative.

Many of us remain in situations that don't serve us. We allow ourselves to believe that things aren't as bad as they seem. However, everyone is born with a **conscience**. Consider the famous concept of an angel on one shoulder and a demon on the other. We all have access to the voice that could guide us away from a bad decision.

How many times is too many times? If you never want to do something again, stand **firm** in that. To eliminate future regrets, remember past mistakes. Avoidable mistakes tend to leave scabs that turn into scars. The beautiful thing about a scar is that it symbolizes survival. Don't feel bad about yesterday, just focus on outdoing it.

WORDS

Holding your tongue is probably one of the hardest things to do. Most people listen to respond instead of listening to understand. After all, having the last word feels rather good, doesn't it? The only problem with this is that the need to have the last word is a bit **egotistical**. It implies that the conversation can't end unless YOU have the final say.

Treat your words like **currency**. If you can't afford the outcome, don't say it. Know that the way you say something is just as important as what you said. Not only do your words influence your tone of voice, but both influence the response you receive. The transference of energy through words is enormously powerful, and it can make or break a conversation.

The person that is speaking deserves the same respect that you require. The notion of sticks and stones breaking bones, but words never hurting is completely false. Being careless with words will always **backfire**. Never take for granted the ability to speak. I challenge you to continue with the knowledge that what you say could change a life.

APOLOGIES

I wonder if you cringed when you read this topic. Nobody, and I mean NOBODY likes to apologize. Many people can bring themselves to do it, but it's not something anyone actually enjoys. Saying sorry simply means that **humility** has control over ego.

It would be easy for me to encourage you not to do things you'd regret. However, that would also just be me reiterating what we've **both** ignored. Life has a way of putting our character and moral compass to the test. I think it's more difficult apologizing to yourself than to others. This means that you have to be **vulnerable** enough to admit having taken part in something that proves you being flawed.

The truth is, we're all going to have to say sorry to someone at some point. Whether it is to ourselves or others, apologizing plays a vital role in evolution. Healing is much easier when the air has been cleared. Never apologize from an unloving place. Apologize because you understand how it feels to be **human**.

SOMETIMES IT'S YOU

No one likes admitting when they're wrong. Some call it being prideful, while others consider it absolutely embarrassing. The only thing worse than knowing you're wrong is **refusing** to do something about it. This doesn't always include apologizing.

Everyone won't get the opportunity to make amends. I'm sure you've learned that actions speak louder than words. If you come to realize where you went wrong, make it a goal not to turn that action into a pattern. You don't have to repeat what you can't take back.

Learn to come to terms with the fact that sometimes it's **you**. Sometimes you aren't the victim. Sometimes it's what you allowed.

Sometimes it's what you caused. Just be sure to remember that *sometimes* is temporary.

FORGIVENESS

It's one thing to be hurt, but it's another to hold on to it. Some of us wear unforgiveness like a pair of glasses. When your vision stems from resentment, and you view everything through a bitter lens, you prohibit yourself from seeing clearly. Choosing to not forgive is **damaging** to your well-being.

This is not to say that everyone you forgive deserves a spot in your life. We just have to use wisdom and common sense when determining a person's placement. When actions turn into life-altering results, an unexpected shift takes place. Whether it is prayer, therapy, or even self-discovery, get through how you feel healthily. You deserve the joy of freeing your mind!

We can't avoid being hurt just as much as we can't promise not to hurt. Forgiveness is important so that you can be **free**. Whatever holds you back can't help you. If you're having difficulty forgiving, know that there is **peace** on the other side of letting it go.

GROWTH

TESTS

Have you ever been unexpectedly **tested**? It's as though you could be doing so well and then BAM! Here comes your trigger. Somewhere in the world, someone just pushed the button that ignites old versions of you. There is nothing more annoying than this, especially when you've been succeeding at restraint.

When pursuing growth, it's common to set a goal declaring that you'll stop a particular habit. It's also common to assume that making this declaration erases all chances for slip-ups. My friend, be

fair to yourself. Give yourself a chance to be human for messing up, and an even better chance by starting over.

A setback doesn't have to mean you'll stay back. Many tests will present themselves as you **pursue** growth. They will become easier to manage if you change the way you view them. You aren't really growing if you aren't being tested. A student only passes the course by proving to have learned the lesson.

LESSONS

There is a saying that I'm most sure you've heard. Many people have suggested that everything happens for a **reason.** I don't know about you, but I usually only hear this when things have taken a turn for the worst. Most people say this when they don't know what else to say.

Although this common phrase can seem insensitive, it possesses so much wisdom. There is indeed a **lesson** behind every circumstance. While you may not always forget an experience, you certainly can learn from it. The matters of life are really matters of knowledge.

Allow yourself the space to be a student. Whether something goes wrong or right, its occurrence was supposed to teach you a lesson. The spoiler alert is that it will happen **again** if you don't receive what it tried to offer. Being open to the teacher in experience will only make you better.

LETTING GO

If you're holding on to something that no longer exists in your life, it's time to **let it go**. We cannot look ahead and behind at the same time. Doing this only confuses your current direction. It is important to let seasons change while allowing yourself to do the same.

We tend to be addicted to what was, whether it consisted of good or bad. This could be a former relationship, milestone, disappointment, or even the person you used to be. Have you ever met someone obsessed with their **past**? It's as though their future could never compare to their previous experiences.

One thing we all must master is the art of letting go. This is one of the secret **ingredients** of self-care. You harm yourself when you allow the past to hold you hostage. Move on, my friend. Good things never happen just once.

PEACE

Storms have a way of **disturbing** bodies of water, but they always go back to being still when the storm is over. The wind has a way of moving branches, but a deeply rooted tree remains still when the wind passes. These are examples of knowing who you are and remaining calm during chaos. The only way to remain calm is to be at **peace** with the way life goes.

Pursuing peace is not always easy. You first have to understand that it's something you deserve. You were not created to be stressed. Have you ever noticed how people usually desire to vacation in more beautiful, tropical climates? This is because those climates represent **relaxation**. Relaxation represents peace.

Never allow anyone or anything to disturb your peace. You may not be able to catch the next flight to Jamaica, but you can certainly have a relaxed mind. When peace is disturbed, the focus is disrupted. Don't let anything or anyone prevent you from experiencing serenity. The next time something tries to negatively shift your mood, remember the tree and be still.

HAPPINESS

Happiness doesn't just knock on your door; you must go **find** it. Once you find it, you must put in work to keep it. Those who have obtained it will tell you that it is a choice. As easy as it is to be negative is as hard as it is to stay positive.

Most people wait for things to happen before they claim to be happy. Others **make** things happen so that happiness will just be there. Why wait on something you should pursue? What's given to you may not last, but you'll do all you can to keep something you created.

Consider relationships and why they either thrive or fail. The pursuit is why they form, but the **effort** is how they remain. Your relationship with happiness is one of the most important that will ever exist. Never assume that happiness will last forever. Just go get it back if it leaves.

YOU

MISPERCEPTION

What happens when people just don't **get** you? I'm sure you've seen quotes that stress how people's opinion of you is none of your business. How people view you should not outweigh the way you view yourself. The more confident you grow in who you are and what you do is what will lessen the impact of what others have to say.

The truth is that you just won't vibe with the entire world. There is no way everyone you know will come to understand the **totality** of what you possess. We waste a lot of time trying to prove ourselves to those who are committed to their **misperception** of us. Sadly, we allow those who misunderstand us to affect us more than those who do. This is simply torture that no one needs.

Know who you are, love who you are, and BE WHO YOU ARE. Begin to view misperception as an **illusion**. Opinions that make you question your existence are irrelevant. If you're good with you, then that's all that matters. How you perceive yourself is what you will essentially attract into your life.

COMPARISON

If you didn't see it every day on social media, you might be a little more **self-motivated**. We are living in a time where boasting about your accomplishments online is the norm. It's almost as though someone is not succeeding if they aren't posting about it. It can also appear that they're thriving if they do choose to post. Never program your mind to believe either assumption.

Have you ever been in an environment where one of your peers seemed to have it all together? This tends to stand out more in seasons of **insecurity**. As a result, it causes you to dress up envy as admiration. You'd love to be happy for them, but it's hard because deep down, you aren't happy with yourself.

People choose what to show just as much as they choose what to keep to themselves. Be careful of living **vicariously** through others when they only show the good stuff. Focus on being the best at what you do. When you're **confident** with your pace, comparison turns into congratulations.

GUILT

Have you ever felt bad about something you couldn't change? Perhaps certain actions led to this feeling. As a result, there is a never-ending reminder of poor decision making that seems to haunt you every day. This reoccurrence can cause you to feel like you'll never be able to move forward. We call this **guilt**.

Guilt is a suffocating **disease** that will eat you alive if you let it. Just as we accumulate complications from not minding our health, guilt is a result of not minding our actions. I suggest a 3-step solution to handling guilt. Acknowledge and make amends with your mistake, detach yourself from its urges, and move forward.

You must realize that each day you wake up is a new **opportunity** for you to give life your best. Guilt is not your fate! You can learn from it more than you can hurt from it. Someone already mastered the responsibility of being perfect so that you wouldn't have to. Don't let the guilt of your past overpower the grace that your future has in store for you.

SELF CONTROL

If you know that doing something is a bad idea, why do it? Every once and a while, we tend to gravitate toward things that aren't good for us. There seems to be something enticing about living on the edge. The downside of an edge is that if you fall, it'll be pretty **hard** to get up.

Haven't we all given in to temptation? It feels great for a moment, but the moment soon fades. Nothing is worse than **temporary** pleasure. If you notice, temptation only exists where weakness resides. This says to me that I'll turn out stronger if I resist.

It is important to realize the power of **self-control**. This is where strength meets sanity before weakness meets regret. If it's difficult to resist, then it just isn't worth it. Whatever loses your attention becomes a thing of the past. What if your future was based on your self-control?

SELF WORTH

If someone said you were worth everything, would you believe them? Only you know the answer to this question. Your worth should not be determined by a person's ability or inability to see you. No one is responsible for your happiness except you. When you ignore the self-work, then you damage the **self-worth**.

The fact that you exist should be reason enough to know that you're **special**. The way you've survived life shows that you have purpose. No mistake or lapse in judgment could amount to the good that is still inside of you. At the very least, the person you see in the mirror is a reflection of God himself. If none of this is convincing, then you haven't gotten to know you yet.

Your worth as a human being is **priceless**, but your self-worth is a result of how much you love yourself. Not only is love a noun, but it is also an adjective and a verb. I believe that how the verb caters to the noun determines the adjective. In other words, how you treat yourself is how you'll feel about yourself. Give yourself the love you deserve, and no one will beat you at knowing your worth.

SELF LOVE

You grow in **reverse** when you love yourself last. You are absolutely amazing. The creator doesn't craft rough drafts, so it is important to view oneself as a finished product. We place unnecessary pressure on others to validate us when we can't recognize our own value.

In many cases, loving others is a preferred **distraction** from loving ourselves. It appears it is easier to solidify the company than solitude. Do not miss the opportunity to explore and experience you. The best way to love others is to love you first. If confidence can eliminate insecurity, imagine what self-love can do.

Self-love has the power to **positively** influence every area of your life. When the care you have for yourself is high, nothing or no one can take away from the joy that rests on your self-esteem. Most people's treatment of you reflects how they've interpreted the way you treat yourself. Be fair. You have every reason and right to love you.

IDENTITY

What you do and how you think when no one's watching is who you are. This is how you come to determine your **identity**. No one knows you the way that you know yourself. Only you know if that aligns with the version of you that everyone else sees.

Sometimes a person wants to be who the world **thinks** they are, and sometimes they want to be seen for who they truly are. If you're struggling with identity, my best advice is to be the you that you're **proud** of. If you aren't proud of who you are, remove the acceptance of it. Anyone can change if they genuinely want to. It is never too late to be the dream you.

Visualize your life and decide who you want to be. Remain **authentic** in whoever that is. Life is too short to keep the best you from or to yourself. May who you are represent your character, and may your character represent your identity.

GOD

RELATIONSHIP

The longest-lasting relationship we'll ever have is with **God**. The truth is that life will cause us to cheat and even break up with him on some occasions. However, the best part about God is that he is always interested in working things out. Isn't that what we all want? A relationship with someone who stays even when they have good reason to leave.

The love we share with God is so powerful that it **withstands** everything designed to destroy it. He exudes such an understanding that overpowers our inability to remain consistent. He continues to wake us up, even in seasons where living seems overrated. He gives second chances where first chances were abused. This is the epitome of **unconditional love**.

A relationship with God is so worth it. Getting to know him doesn't have to be boring or intimidating. Trust me, I've learned through experience. Spend some time around nature. Pay attention to the unexplainable wonders of life. Read about him. Take it all in. Talk to him. Learn to be still. Eventually, you'll notice that he's been **everywhere** the whole time.

GRACE

When **grace** is mentioned, it is commonly associated with God. Many people use the term when praying over their food, while others use it to describe the way God loves us when we least deserve it. Let's focus on the latter. There is a love that exists even when we make mistakes. Wow.

It seems to me that one who understands grace can also understand love. A parent displays grace when they choose to react verbally as opposed to physically. A professor extends grace when they offer extra credit to a failing student. God extends grace when he doesn't co-sign our mistakes yet still **forgives** us for them. If we didn't need it, it wouldn't be available. If we didn't deserve it, we wouldn't have it.

Guilt prevails where grace fails. Just as God is gracious toward you, you must be gracious toward yourself. Your *mistakes* are not your identity. Just remember that when you aren't good, God **still** is. That, my friend, is grace.

GOD'S INPUT

Oftentimes, God is **calling** us to an avenue we're afraid to explore. You can go through life doing everything your way then get thrown off when you add him to the mix. The plans we have for ourselves are not always God's plans for us. This doesn't have to mean that you're striving toward something bad. It just means that your focus gets **displaced** when he isn't a part of the planning.

Seeking God in all you do is an **essential** part of decision making. He can confirm or deny your next move. He is also capable of letting you figure it all out if you don't want his help. God doesn't force his input; he just wishes you would put him in.

Your choice may be good, but it may not be God. A move by you may affect a few, but a move by him could **impact** many. Make sure he owns the key to the doors you want opened. That's the only way you'll stay inside.

CONVICTION

I almost didn't write this chapter, but I know someone needs it. Ironically, this topic perfectly describes not wanting to do something but knowing you should. **Conviction** is a strong word that has a strong effect. The way I would describe it is that it is a feeling you get when you're operating outside of the will of God for your life. To make it even more clear, the only way you'll feel convicted is if you have a **relationship** with him.

There is a difference between feeling bad and feeling convicted. When you feel bad, it eventually goes away. When you feel convicted, the feeling will nearly bully you until you address it. We must start minding our actions and stop ignoring our convictions. You feel uneasy because something needs to **change**.

I used to be afraid of conviction until I viewed it as a **secret weapon**. It is simply God's way of disciplining me before I ruin my own life. You see, we'll never have peace by embracing things that aren't good for us. Conviction doesn't take away the fun, it redefines it.

GOD IDEAS

Have you ever received an idea that didn't come from you or another human? I'm talking about the kind that would have made zero sense if it hadn't just appeared in your mind. Moments like this are usually **intentional**. I like to think of these ideas as God's suggestion for what you should do next.

What seems confusing can turn into purpose if you take it seriously. There is a scripture that says, "When someone has been **given** much, much will be required in return; and when someone has been **entrusted** with much, even more will be required."(Luke 12:48 NLT) This is simply to say that if God gives you an ability, you should use it, but when he ASSIGNS you a task, you should do it. The blueprint will be provided when you accept the assignment.

There is no satisfaction in ignoring your potential. Never let go of an idea that came from God. He gave it to you on purpose. Disappointed is the man that only sees things in his head. Happy is the man that sees things through.

PERSPECTIVE PRAYER

"Heavenly Father, I want to start off by saying thank you. Thank you for creating me and having me in mind for this world. I have to admit that sometimes I'm confused by your plans for me. Please help me to determine the difference between my plans and yours. I ask that you forgive me for any time I misinterpreted your love. I am grateful for the blessings and lessons you've allowed. When it comes to my life, I want all parts of how you see it for me. I love you, and I thank you. Amen."

THE PATH

I saw a path that looked like me, so that's the way I went,

But halfway down the path, I saw another path that bent.

You see, the path I took was so familiar it felt great,

So why would I get off and join a path I saw too late?

I stood there, and I thought about the way my life had gone,

I'd played it safe according to the path that I was on.

Suddenly the wind blew my things in the air,

And that's the day I realized my path was over there.

-B.Lin

ACKNOWLEDGEMENTS

*I want to thank God for giving me purpose, my loving parents Andre`
& Pamela Linton for putting me in programs that cultivated my gift,
my sister Arika for being a constant support, Vanessa Parker for
holding me accountable, Erica Stewart for being a voice of reason,
Kristen Turner for a life-changing conversation, Billy Montgomery for
his mentorship, Kristen R. Harris & The Scribe Tribe for bringing my
vision to life, and my family and friends that have supported me along
the way.*

ABOUT THE AUTHOR

Brittanye "B.Lin" Linton is a singer/songwriter from Chicago, IL. Always a wordsmith, B.Lin prides herself on having the same birthday as William Shakespeare. As an alum of thee Kenwood Academy, this Bronco found power in her words at an early age. Her confidence soared when she became an HBCU graduate of Dillard University.

Upon graduating, B.Lin released two musical projects. A car assembler by day, she finds inspiration to keep her dreams at the forefront of her mind. As a new author, she seeks to awaken the dreamer to remind them that how you see it is how it will be.

Photo by Dwight Thomas Photography

Made in the USA
Columbia, SC
31 August 2021